Charlie B
The Therapy Dog

by
DJ Clancy

Illustrated by
Joshua Allen

AuthorHouse™ LLC
1663 Liberty Drive
Bloomington, IN 47403
www.authorhouse.com
Phone: 1-800-839-8640

Published by AuthorHouse 04/07/2014

ISBN: 978-1-4969-0358-7 (sc)
        978-1-4969-0359-4 (e)

Library of Congress Control Number: 2014906511

Any people depicted in stock imagery provided by Thinkstock are models,
and such images are being used for illustrative purposes only.
Certain stock imagery © Thinkstock.

This book is printed on acid-free paper.

authorHOUSE®

Charlie B

The Therapy Dog

A basket full of puppies, how cute are we.

I'm over here. Pick me, pick me!

Which one will she choose? Spotted, brown, or black?

Oh, wait! She sees me. I'm in the back.

I have the big brown eyes. Yup, she is picking me!

And she's going to call me her Charlie B.

Follow me, Mom. Come this way.

We'll stay together so I don't lose my way.

Let's run in the rain. Let's walk on the beach.

Who knows what we'll discover? Who knows who we'll meet?

"Meow!" What's that? I say.

"I'm Samantha, the cat, and I live here too,

so we have to get along, me and you.

You are a dog, and I am a cat.

You like to play ball, but I don't like that.

You like to swim, and I hate that.

You take walks. I take naps.

Yes, we are different, and that's okay.

We'll be good friends, living day by day."

Look, Mom, over there–

a dog like me, only he looks like a bear.

He sure looks different, and that's okay.

I know we'll be best friends as we run along and play.

When I was a puppy, I had some little jobs, a few.

But now I'm all grown-up, doing what I was meant to do.

All my friends are pointing as they look at me and laugh.

They say my forehead's pink and that I need a bath.

It's pink because I'm a therapy dog with a special job to do.

When people see me coming, I get hugs and kisses too.

It's off to the hospital; time to go to work.

I make people smile when they are hurt.

Come on, Mom. It's time for school!

The children want to meet me. They think I'm very cool.

I love my job. I really do.

Then I do my tricks as they all yell, "We love you too!"

I'm tired now and want to sleep—

to dream and to remember

all the fun we had and all our days together.

Oh, what a ride we had, you and me.

Always and forever, Mom.

Love,

your Charlie B.

CPSIA information can be obtained
at www.ICGtesting.com
Printed in the USA
BVOW10s0857191016
465438BV00009B/121/P